JOSEPH CAMPBELL ON MYTH & MYTHOLOGY

Edited by
Richard L. Sartore
Writer and Educational Consultant

UNIVERSITY
PRESS OF
AMERICA

Lanham • New York • London

Copyright © 1994 by
University Press of America®, Inc.
4720 Boston Way
Lanham, Maryland 20706

Library of Congress Cataloging-in-Publication Data

Joseph Campbell on myth and mythology / edited by Richard L.
Sartore.
p.   cm.
Includes bibliographical references.
1. Campbell, Joseph, 1904–   —Contributions in concept of myth.
2. Myth.   3. Mythology.   I. Sartore, Richard L.
BL304.J67   1993   291.1'3'092—dc20   93–20263 CIP

ISBN 0–8191–9080–2 (cloth : alk. paper)
ISBN 0–8191–9081–0 (pbk. : alk. paper)

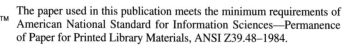

The paper used in this publication meets the minimum requirements of
American National Standard for Information Sciences—Permanence
of Paper for Printed Library Materials, ANSI Z39.48–1984.

To Zagreus who taught me that-
once I opened up my eyes-
living was an enriching adventure.

ACKNOWLEDGEMENTS

My gratitude is extended to the numerous people who were so kind in sharing their time and knowledge to make this book possible. First and foremost, I would like thank my friend and mentor, the late Bill "Zagreus" Rawlin. Every person should have the luxury of knowing someone like Bill. Through his tireless efforts and wealth of knowledge, he made the words of Joseph Campbell an obvious reality. The drawing of Joseph Campbell was done by Stephen Pitkin. During the course of his art work, he became interested in the mythological ramifications espoused by Campbell.

Stu Horn gave a critical analysis of the manuscript over months of writing. Without his constructive comments, critiques and overall editorial impressions, the writing would lack the readability inherent within these pages. Many thanks to Lawrence Crutchley who spent hours of his time developing charts and reading the manuscript. His input is evident throughout the work.

There are other people to thank such as Eileen Baker who did a great deal of typing and reading for this manuscript. Eileen's daughter, Kristin, also lent a hand in organizing the material and typing the end product. Sue Karbowski and Kathleen Riley gave of their time in an unwavering and enthusiastic manner. Their advice was sincerely appreciated. In all, I would like to gratefully acknowledge those contributors who measurably enriched this book.

CONTENTS

I made my song a coat
Covered with embroideries
Out of old mythologies
From heel to throat;
But the fools caught it,
Wore it in the world's eyes
As though they'd wrought it.
Song, let them take it,
For there's more enterprise
In walking naked.

A COAT

-W. B. Yeats-

INTRODUCTION

When a friend first introduced me to the works of Joseph Campbell little did I realize that my involvement would expand to an adventure. The first book read was THE HERO WITH A THOUSAND FACES. It was a magnificent writing representing one in a series of provocative thoughts that sent me on my own journey to discover how Campbell arrived at his fascinating concepts.

As a foremost American mythologist, Joseph Campbell served on the faculty of Sarah Lawrence College from 1934 to his retirement in 1972. He studied at Dartmouth College, Columbia University, as well as the Universities of Paris and Munich. Among numerous awards, Campbell received the National Institute of Arts and Letters Award for Contribution to Creative Literature for his book THE HERO WITH A THOUSAND FACES. In 1985 he earned the Medal of Honor for Literature from the National Arts Club. His interview with Bill Moyers on the PBS series entitled THE POWER OF MYTH, further expanded his fame. Until his death in 1987, he was a popular spokesperson for his unique views on mythology and life.

Recent modern American thought glorified Newtonic rational-linear science which held that all behavior could be scientifically explained and ignored the metaphorical nature of the world. Myths were treated as quaint primitive stories.

Even in theology the trend was to demythologize the sacred scriptures and religious processes (i.e. leaving Latin out of the Mass and removing saints from religious practice). Into this arena came Joseph Campbell who, along with Mircea Eliade, challenged the death of mythology at the hands of rational-linear thought. He demonstrated how myths were as important today as they were in the past and subsequently diagramed a "remything process" that each individual could utilize in the search for "bliss". Evident in his writings is the message that mythology permeates each human life and significantly affects behavior from birth to death. To be consonant with Campbell's style, and for the sake of economy, the hero/heroine is usually described with a male pronoun. The author recognizes that the female pronoun is equally valid.

In regard to the initial chart labeled ARCHITECTURE OF CAMPBELL'S THEORIES, his early writings, including THE FLIGHT OF THE WILD GANDER and A SKELETON KEY TO FINNEGAN'S WAKE, signaled the themes of the "hero" and "bliss" which eventually formed the basis of his definitive statements on mythology. He clearly explains the Primitive, Traditional and Creative Mythologies that become the foundation forunderstanding the "hero" and "bliss" concepts. Therefore, in order to comprehend how the "hero" and "bliss" themes evolved, we must first trace the growth of Campbell's thinking.

The hub of Campbell's philosophy can be viewed in the chart (ARCHITECTURE OF CAMPBELL'S THEORIES). The early years began with reporting work and telling mythical stories. Later there was an expanded dimension that involved careful interpretation and integration based in world cultures. Ultimately a refinement occurred and the notion of "hero" and "bliss" emerged. The "hero" concept was further buttressed by writings that substantiated earlier theories.

After a comprehensive examination of the book by Campbell named THE HERO WITH A THOUSAND FACES, I decided that it would be fragmentary to excerpt select passages. To maintain the integrity of what is expressed about the hero, the flow of the entire book is essential. The words and myths are so dependent upon each other that it would be unfair to draw direct quotes from a gold mine of information. The entire text would require quoting to do an adequate job. Hence the reader is encouraged to examine the complete writing.

The more one reads about THE HERO WITH A THOUSAND FACES, the more one is swept into learning about Joseph Campbell's views on mythology and the hero's journey. The path of life that leads to adventure is created by the hero.

Examples of myths throughout history are given in THE HERO

WITH A THOUSAND FACES. Traditionally, the path is laid out for the person and pursued accordingly. T. S. Eliot describes in THE WASTE LAND that a tract of life is often determined by someone else's standards. On the contrary, the hero's path is actually contrived by the person in order to seek an important adventure. The hero goes beyond the lifestyle characteristic of his traditional culture. A set pattern, a predetermined standard of life, is broken by the hero who goes off and seeks his own adventure. His journey leads to an unknown land where seeming insurmountable obstacles are encountered and suffering ensues. The hero triumphs and is reborn. He returns to his people armed with new insights to be shared for all to benefit.

THE HERO WITH A THOUSAND FACES describes some of the multitude of facets involved in successfully achieving the hero's journey. With all the faces of heros, three points surface. The first is the hero who leaves his society and travels to some unexplored adventure only to return and proclaim that this new reality is not for him. His original culture remains the best. The second is the person who leaves his cultural orientation and seeks the unfamiliar only to return to say that he would like to stay in his originating society but he has a few things that were learned on his journey and would like to apply them to his culture. The third type of hero leaves his society altogether and proclaims that it is far better outside his society. Each one of these people have experienced a degree of "bliss" by taking the journey to pursue other worlds. At the end of the final chapter (THE HERO'S JOURNEY AND BEYOND) there is a diagram (THE HERO'S JOURNEY TO BLISS) that charts the hero's adventure.

No matter what book is read or what myth is pursued, two considerations are ever present. The connection between the "hero" and "bliss" is evident for they both represent a keystone component to all his works. Given the architecture of Campbell, two modes constantly appear. When we examine primitive, traditional and creative mythology we find that the last stage of creative mythology leading to bliss actually, with time, evolves back into a traditional mythology. What was creative at one point is no longer applicable in the future. Also, creative mythology produces parallels. For instance, one creative religion may engender and spawn several others.

Among all his works, the four volume series THE MASKS OF GOD surveyed the world's mythology and buttressed the idea of a unified monomyth. As indicated in PRIMITIVE MYTHOLOGY, in the early phase of primitive society, starting with the Bronze Age, man had the basic set of religious beliefs and responses about the universe. Hunting and gathering were the mainstay of prehistoric societies and what and how they believed was based on these daily activities. The second work in the series, THE MASKS OF GOD, was ORIENTAL MYTHOLOGY. Here the myths of the East were covered including those of China, Egypt, India and Japan. Campbell addresses the notion of reincarnation and the part played by the individual.

The third volume is OCCIDENTAL MYTHOLOGY. Western religious belief is followed down through the ages. A strong contrast is made between the East and West. And finally, in THE MASKS OF GOD: CREATIVE MYTHOLOGY Campbell directs his attention toward modern day myths. He talks about developing a new mythology that is applicable to humans of contemporary society rather than depending on myths of the past created by anonymous authors. I saw this as a change from perceiving a myth from a past external source and changing it to developing a myth within ourselves, a personal myth. These four volumes are core material to the Campbell mythological perspective.

Throughout his writings, Campbell effectively drew a mythological distinction between East and West. Crucial "unanswerable questions" on virgin births, life, death, reincarnation and gods, are constantly addressed. Thus mythology becomes a psychological response to those "unanswerable questions" that exist in all cultures. Many of his works are steeped in the writings of Jung, Joyce, Mann and Schopenhauer.

Ever since his interest with mythologies of the American Indian, Campbell's pursuits expanded to include all sides of the globe. Mythology was previously viewed as solely a historical event with trivial substance. However, Campbell successfully coupled myth and mythology to religion and hence formed a giant poem that was in fact a slice of life. Mythology actually provides insights into "how" and "why" people thought the way they did. We come to find that, according to Campbell, despite the seeming difference in what we see as mythology of certain specific cultures, they are universal concepts. The only difference in these so-called "concepts" is how they translate into mythological language.

Joseph Campbell was both a brilliant scholar and a popular individual. He was scholarly in that he could discuss matters in diverse fields. On the other hand, he was comfortable with individuals not typically labeled scholars when he conveyed his sentiments. Perhaps the statement by Michael Toms in AN OPEN LIFE (p. 14) best describes Campbell's impact: "his words were like water to a thirsty mind".

Richard L. Sartore
Clifton Park, New York

Joseph Campbell
1904-1987

ARCHITECTURE OF CAMPBELL'S THEORIES

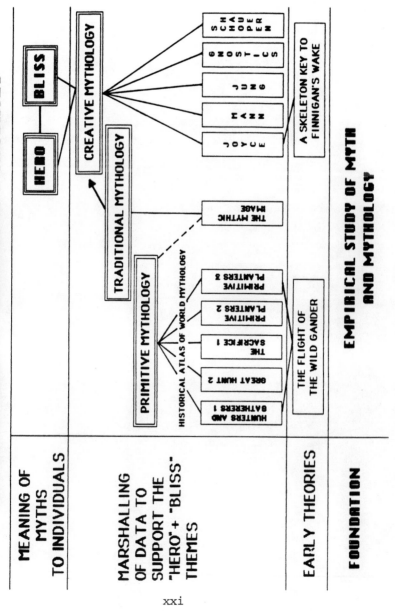

MEANING OF MYTHS TO INDIVIDUALS	MARSHALLING OF DATA TO SUPPORT THE "HERO" + "BLISS" THEMES	EARLY THEORIES	FOUNDATION

HERO   BLISS

CREATIVE MYTHOLOGY

TRADITIONAL MYTHOLOGY

PRIMITIVE MYTHOLOGY

JOYCE   MANN   JUNG   GNOSTICS   SCHAUPER

A SKELETON KEY TO FINNIGAN'S WAKE

THE MYTHIC IMAGE

HISTORICAL ATLAS OF WORLD MYTHOLOGY

HUNTERS AND GATHERERS 1   GREAT HUNT 2   THE SACRIFICE 1   PRIMITIVE PLANTERS 2   PRIMITIVE PLANTERS 3

THE FLIGHT OF THE WILD GANDER

EMPIRICAL STUDY OF MYTH AND MYTHOLOGY

xxi

MYTHOLOGICAL TIMELINE

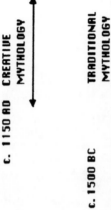

600,000 BC c. 40,000 BC c. 2500 BC
(CRO-MAGNON) (Crude Script)

c. 1500 BC

c. 1150 AD   CREATIVE
MYTHOLOGY

TRADITIONAL
MYTHOLOGY

PRIMITIVE
MYTHOLOGY

INCEPTION OF:
Poeisis
Mask
Metaphor

THE PROCESS OF CHANGE FROM TRADITIONAL TO CREATIVE MYTHOLOGY

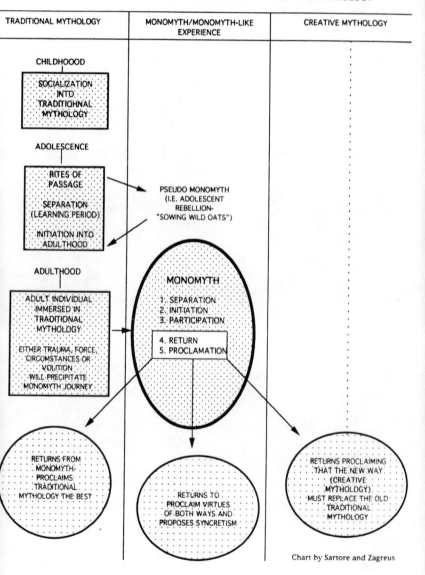

Chart by Sartore and Zagreus

CHAPTER I

MYTH AND MYTHOLOGY

What is a myth? The dictionary definition of a myth would be stories about gods. So then you have to ask the next question: What is a god? A god is a personification of a motivating power or a value system that functions in human life and in the universe - the powers of your own body and of nature. The myths are metaphorical of spiritual potentiality in the human being, and the same powers that animate our life animate the life of the world. But also there are myths and gods that have to do with specific societies or the patron deities of the society. In other words, there are two totally different orders of mythology. There is the mythology that relates you to your nature and to the natural world, of which you're a part. And there is the mythology that is strictly sociological, linking you to a particular society. You are not simply a natural man, you are a member of a particular group. In the history of European mythology, you can see the interaction of these two systems. Usually the socially oriented system is of a monadic people who are moving around, so you learn that's where your center is, in that group. The nature-oriented mythology would be of an earth-cultivating people...

Now, the biblical tradition is a socially oriented mythology. Nature is condemned. In the nineteenth century, scholars thought of mythology and ritual as an attempt to control nature. But that is magic, not mythology or religion. Nature religions are not attempts to control nature but to help put yourself in accord with it. But when nature is thought of as evil, you don't put yourself in accord with it, you control it, or try to, and hence the tension, the anxiety, the cutting down of forests, the annihilation of native people. And the accent here separates us from nature. (PM, pp. 22-24)

The individual has to find an aspect of myth that relates to his own life. Myth basically serves four functions. The first is the mystical function - that is the one I've been speaking about, realizing what a wonder the universe is, and what a wonder you are, and experiencing awe before this mystery. Myth opens the world to the dimension of mystery, to the realization of the mystery that underlies all forms. If you lose that, you don't have a mythology. If mystery is manifest through all things, the universe becomes, as it were, a holy picture. You are always addressing the transcendent mystery through the conditions of the world...

The second is a cosmological dimension, the dimension with which science is concerned - showing you what the shape of the universe is, but showing it in such a way that the mystery again comes through. Today we tend to think that scientists have all the answers. But the great ones tell us, "No, we haven't got all the answers. We're telling you how it works - but what is it?" You strike a match, what's a fire? You can tell me about oxidation, but that doesn't tell me a thing...

The third function is the sociological one - supporting and validating a certain social order. And here's where the myths vary enormously from place to place. You can have a whole mythology for polygamy, a whole mythology for monogamy. Either one's okay. It depends on where you are. It is this sociological function of myth that has taken over in our world - and it is out of date...

But there is a fourth function of myth, and this is the one that I think everyone must try today to relate to - and that is the pedagogical function, of how to live a human lifetime under any circumstances. Myths can teach you that. (PM, p. 31)

The functions normally served by a properly operating mythology. They are in my judgement, four.

The first is what I have called the mystical function: to waken and maintain in the individual a sense of awe and gratitude in relation to the mystery dimension of the universe, not so that he lives in fear of it, but so that he recognizes that he participates in it, since the mystery of being is the mystery of his own deep being as well...

The second function of a living mythology is to offer an image of the universe that will be in accord with the knowledge of the time, the sciences and the fields of action of the folk to whom the mythology is addressed...

The third function of a living mythology is to validate, support, and imprint the norms of a given specific moral order, that, namely, of the society in which the individual is to live. And the fourth is to guide him, stage by stage, in health, strength, and harmony of spirit, through the whole foreseeable course of a useful life.   (MLB, pp. 221-22)

An exactly comparable biological function is served in our own species by a mythology, which is no less an indispensable biological organ, no less a nature product, though apparently something else. Like the nest of a bird, a mythology is fashioned of materials drawn from the local environment, apparently altogether consciously, but according to an architecture unconsciously dictated from within. And it simply does not matter whether its comforting, fostering, guiding images would be appropriate for an adult. It is not intended for adults. Its first function is to foster an unready psyche to maturity, preparing it to face its world. (MLB, pp. 222-23)

Fairy tales are told for entertainment. You've got to distinguish between the myths that have to do with the serious matter of living life in terms of the order of society and of nature, and stories with some of those same motifs that are told for entertainment. But even though there's a happy ending for most fairy tales, on the way to the happy ending , typical mythological motifs occur - for example, the motif of being in deep trouble and then hearing a voice or having somebody come to help you out...

Fairy tales are for children. Very often they're about a little girl who doesn't want to grow up to be a woman. At the crisis of that threshold crossing she's balking. So she goes to sleep until the prince comes through all the barriers and gives her a reason to think it might be nice on the other side after all. (PM, p. 138)

Greek and Latin and biblical literature used to be a part of everyone's education. Now, when these were dropped, a whole tradition of Occidental mythological information was lost. It used to be that these stories were in the minds of the people. When the story is in your mind, then you see its relevance to something happening in your own life. It gives you perspective on what's happening to you. With the loss of that, we've really lost something because we don't have a comparable literature to take its place. These bits of information from ancient times, which have to do with the themes that have supported human life, built civilizations, and informed religions over the millennia, have to do with deep inner problems, inner mysteries, inner thresholds of passage, and if you don't know what the guidelines are along the way, you have to work it out yourself. But once this subject catches you, there is such a feeling, from one or another of these traditions, of information of a deep, rich, life-vivifying sort that you don't want to give it up. (PM, p. 4)

Mythology--and therefore civilization--is a poetic, supernormal image, conceived, like all poetry, in depth, but susceptible of interpretation on various levels. The shallowest minds see in it the local scenery; the deepest, the foreground of the void; and between are all the stages of the Way from the ethnic to the elementary idea, the local to the universal being, which is Everyman, as he both knows and is afraid to know. For the human mind in the polarity of the male and female modes of experience, in its passages from infancy to adulthood and old age, in its toughness and tenderness, and its continuing dialogue with the world, is the ultimate mytholgenic zone--the creator and destroyer, the slave and yet the master, of all the gods.   (MPM, p. 472)

This recognition of mortality and the requirement to transcend it is the first great impulse to mythology. And along with this there runs another realization; namely, that the social group into which the individual has been borne, which nourishes and protects him and which, for the greater part of his life, he must himself help to nourish and protect, was flourishing long before his own birth and will remain after he is gone. That is to say, not only does the individual member of our species, conscious of himself as such, face death, but he confronts also the necessity to adapt himself to whatever order of life may happen to be that of the community into which he has been born, this being an order of life superordinated to his own, a super-organism into which he must allow himself to be absorbed, and through participation in which he will come to know the life that transcends death. In every one of the mythological systems that in the long course of history and prehistory have been propagated in the various zones and quarters of this earth, these two fundamental realizations--of the inevitability of individual death and the endurance of the social order--have been combined symbolically and constitute the nuclear structuring force of the rites and, thereby, the society.   (MLB, p. 20-21)

There has been from earliest times the idea that war (of one kind or another) is not only inevitable and good but also the normal and most exhilarating mode of social action of civilized mankind, the waging of war being the normal delight, as well as duty, of kings. A monarch neither engaged in nor preparing to be engaged in war would be, according to this way of thinking, a fool: a "paper tiger." (MLB, p. 203)

Modern scholarship, systematically comparing the myths and rites of mankind, has found just about everywhere legends of virgins giving birth to heroes who die and are resurrected. India is chock-full of such tales, and its towering temples, very like the Aztec ones, represent again our many-storied cosmic mountain, bearing Paradise on its summit and with horrible hells beneath. The Buddhists and the Jains have similar ideas. And, looking backward into the pre-Christian past, we discover in Egypt the mythology of the slain and resurrected Osiris; in Mesopotamia, Tammuz; in Syria, Adonis; and in Greece, Dionysos: all of which furnished models to the early Christians for the representations of Christ. (MLB, p. 8)

The hunter is always directed outward to the animal. His life depends on the relationship to the animals. His mythology is outward turned. But the planting mythology, which has to do with the cultivation of the plant, the planting of the seed, the death of the seed, so to say, and the coming of the new plant, is more inward turned. With the hunters, the animals inspired the mythology. When a man wanted to gain power and knowledge, he would go into the forest and fast and pray, and an animal would come and teach him...

With the planters, the plant world is the teacher. The plant world is identical in its life sequence with the life of man. So you see, there's an inward relationship there. (PM, p. 102)

It is apparent in the light of the findings of archaeology that during the first and primitive stages of the history of our species there was a general centrifugal movement of peoples into distance, to all sides, with the various populations becoming increasingly separated, each developing its own applications and associated interpretation of the shared universal motifs; whereas, since we are all now being brought together again in this   mighty present period of world transport and communication, those differences are fading. The old differences separating one system from another now are becoming less and less important, less and less easy to define. (MLB, p. 22)

Today we know -- and know right well -- that there was never anything of the kind: no Garden of Eden anywhere on this earth, no time when the serpent could talk, no prehistoric "Fall," no exclusion from the garden, no universal Flood, no Noah's Ark. The entire history on which our leading Occidental religions have been founded is an anthology of fictions. But these are fictions of a type that have had -- curiously enough -- a universal vogue as the founding legends of other religions, too. Their counterparts have turned up everywhere -- and yet, there was never such a garden, serpent, tree, or deluge.   (MLB, p. 23-24)

What I would suggest is that by comparing a number from different parts of the world and differing traditions, one might arrive at an understanding of their force, their source and possible sense. For they are not historical. That much is clear. They speak, therefore, not of outside events but of themes of the imagination. And since they exhibit features that are actually universal, they must in some way represent features of our general racial imagination, permanent features of the human spirit -- or, as we say today, of the psyche. (MLB, p. 24)

Taken as referring not to any geographical scene, but to a landscape of the soul, that Garden of Eden would have to be within us. Yet our conscious minds are unable to enter it and enjoy there the taste of eternal life, since we have already tasted of the knowledge that has thrown us out of the garden, pitched us away from our own center, so that we now judge things in those terms and experience only good and evil instead of eternal life -- which, since the enclosed garden is within us, must already be ours, even though unknown to our conscious personalities. That would seem to be the meaning of the myth when read, not as prehistory, but as referring to man's inward spiritual state. (MLB, p. 25)

Nor does it matter from the standpoint of a comparative study of symbolic forms whether Christ or the Buddha ever actually lived and performed the miracles associated with their teachings. The religious literatures of the world abound in counterparts of those two great lives. And what one may learn from them all, finally, is that the savior, the hero, the redeemed one, is the one who has learned to penetrate the protective wall of those fears within, which exclude the rest of us, generally, in our daylight and even our dreamnight thoughts, from all experience of our own and the world's divine ground. The mythologized biographies of such saviors communicate the message of their world-transcending wisdom in world-transcending symbols -- which, ironically, are then generally translated back into such verbalized thoughts as built the interior walls in the first place. (MLB, p. 29)

Heaven and hell are within us, and all the gods are within us. This is the great realization of the Upanishads of India in the ninth century B.C. All the gods, all the heavens, all the worlds, are within us. They are magnified dreams, and dreams are manifestations in image form of the energies of the body in conflict with each other. That is what myth is. (PM, p. 39)

Eternity isn't some later time. Eternity isn't even a long time. Eternity has nothing to do with time. Eternity is that dimension of here and now that all thinking in temporal terms cuts off. And if you don't get it here, you won't get it anywhere. The problem with heaven is that you will be having such a good time there, you won't even think of eternity. You'll just have this unending delight in the beautific vision of God. But the experience of eternity right here and now, in all things, whether thought of as good or as evil, is the function of all life. (PM, p. 67)

The usual marriage in traditional cultures was arranged for by the families. It wasn't a person-to-person decision at all. In India to this day, you have columns in the newspapers of advertisements for wives that are put in by marriage brokers. I remember, in one family that I knew there, the daughter was going to marry. She had never seen the young man she was going to marry, and she would ask her brothers, "Is he tall? Is he dark? Is he light? What?" In the middle ages, that was the kind of marriage that was sanctified by the Church. And so the troubador idea of real person-to-person Amor was very dangerous. (PM, p. 189)

Marriage in the Middle Ages was almost exclusively a social, family concern -- as it has been forever, of course, in Asia, and is to this day for many in the West. One was married according to family arrangements. Particularly in aristocratic circles, young women hardly out of girlhood were married off as political pawns. And the Church, meanwhile, was sacramentalizing such unions with its inappropriately mystical language about the two that were now to be of one flesh, united through love and by God: and let no man put asunder what God hath joined. Any actual experience of love could enter into such a system only as a harbinger of disaster. For not only could one be burned at the stake in punishment for adultery, but, according to current belief, one would also burn forever in Hell. (MLB, p. 162)

The troubadors were very much interested in the psychology of love. And they're the first ones in the West who really thought of love the way we do now - as a person-to-person relationship. (PM, p. 186)

Myth helps you to put your mind in touch with this experience of being alive. It tells you what the experience is. Marriage, for example. What is marriage? The myth tells you what it is. It's the reunion of the separated duad. Originally you were one. You are now two in the world, but the recognition of the spiritual identity is what the marriage is. It's different from a love affair. It has nothing to do with that. It's another mythological plane of experience. When people get married because they think it's a long-time love affair, they'll be divorced very soon, they'll be divorced very soon, because all love affairs end in disappointment. But marriage is recognition of a spiritual identity. If we live a proper life, if our minds are on the right qualities in regarding the person of the opposite sex, we will find our proper male or female counterpart. But if we are distracted by certain sensuous interests, we'll marry the wrong person. By marrying the right person, we reconstruct the image of the incarnate God, and that's what marriage is. (PM, p. 6)

Marriage is a relationship. When you make the

sacrifice in marriage, you're sacrificing not to each other but to unity in a relationship. The Chinese image of the Tao, with the dark and light interacting - that's the relationship of yang and yin, male and female which is what a marriage is. And that's what you have become when you have married. You're no longer this one alone; your identity is in a relationship. Marriage is not a simple love affair, it's an ordeal, and the ordeal is the sacrifice of ego to a relationship in which two have become one. (PM, p. 7)

I would say that if the marriage isn't a first priority in your life, you're not married. The marriage means the two that are one, the two become one flesh. If the marriage lasts long enough, and if you are acquiescing constantly to it instead of to individual personal whim, you come to realize that that is true - the two really are one. (PM, p. 6)

Mythology teaches you what's behind literature and the arts, it teaches you about your own life. It's a great, exciting, life-nourishing subject. Mythology has a great deal to do with the stages of life, the initiation ceremonies as you move from childhood to adult responsibilities, from the unmarried state into the married state. All of those rituals are mythological rites. They have to do with your recognition of the new role that you're in, the process of throwing off the old one and coming out in the new, and entering into a responsible profession.   (PM, pp. 11-12)

On this immediate level of life and structure, myths offer life models. But the models have to be appropriate to the time in which you are living, and our time has changed so fast that what was proper fifty years ago is not proper today. And many of what were thought to be the vices of the past are the necessities of actual life in time, here and now. And that is what we are not doing. The old-time religion belongs to another age, another people, another set of human values, another universe. By going back you throw yourself out of sync with history. Our kids lose their faith in the religions that were taught to them, and they go inside. (PM, p. 13)

People say that what we're all seeking is a meaning for life. I don't think that's what we're really seeking. I think that what we're seeking is an experience of being alive, so that our life experiences on the purely physical plane will have resonances within our own innermost being and reality, so that we actually feel the rapture of being alive. That's what it's all finally about, and that's what these clues help us to find within ourselves. (PM, p. 5)

Mythology is the song. It is the song of the

imagination, inspired by the energies of the body. Once a Zen master stood up before his students and was about to deliver a sermon. And just as he was about to open his mouth, a bird sang. And he said, "The sermon has been delivered."
(PM, p. 22)

Life is, in its very essence and character, a terrible mystery -- this whole business of living by killing and eating. But it is a childish attitude to say no to life with all its pain, to say that this is something that should not have been. (PM, p. 65)

Every mythology has to do with the wisdom of life as related to a specific culture at a specific time. It integrates the individual into his society and the society into the field of nature. it unites the field of nature with my nature. It's a harmonizing force. Our own mythology, for example, is based on the idea of duality: good and evil, heaven and hell. And so our religions tend to be ethical in their accent. Sin and atonement. Right and wrong. (PM, p. 55)

Eternity is beyond all categories of thought. This is an important point in all of the great Oriental religions. We want to think about God. God is a thought. God is a name. God is an idea. But its reference is to something that transcends all thinking. The ultimate mystery of being is beyond all categories of thought. As Kant said, the thing in itself is no thing. It transcends thingness, it goes past anything that could be thought. The best things can't be told because they transcend thought. The second best are misunderstood, because those are the thoughts that are supposed to refer to that which can't be thought about. And myth is that field of reference to what is absolutely transcendent. (PM, p. 49)

All of life is a meditation, most of it unintentional. A lot of people spend most of life in meditating on where their money is coming from and where it's going to go. If you have a family to bring up, you're concerned for the family. These are all very important concerns, but they have to do with physical conditions, mostly. But how are you going to communicate spiritual consciousness to the children if you don't have it yourself? How do you get that? What the myths are for is to bring us into level of consciousness that is spiritual. (PM, p. 14)

I have a feeling that consciousness and energy are the same thing somehow. Where you really see life energy, there's consciousness. Certainly the vegetable world is conscious. And when you live in the woods, as I did as a kid, you can see all these different consciousnesses relating to themselves. There is a plant consciousness and there is an animal consciousness, and we share both these things. You eat certain foods, and the bile knows whether there's something for it to go to work on. The whole process is consciousness. Trying to interpret it in simply mechanistic terms won't work. (PM, p. 14)

You've got the same body, with the same organs and energies, that Cro-Magnon man had thirty thousand years ago. Living a human life in New York City or living a human life in the caves, you go through the same stages of childhood, coming to sexual maturity, transformation of the dependency of childhood into the responsibility of manhood or womanhood, marriage, then failure of the body, gradual loss of its powers, and death. You have the same body, the same bodily experiences, and so you respond to the same images. (PM, p. 37)

We have today to learn to get back into accord with the wisdom of nature and realize again our brotherhood with the animals and with the water and the sea. To say that the divinity informs the world and all things is condemned as pantheism. But pantheism is a misleading word. It suggests that a personal god is supposed to inhabit the world, but that is not the idea at all. The idea is trans-theological. It is of an undefinable, inconceivable mystery, thought of as a power, that is the source and end, and supporting ground of all life and being. (PM, p. 31)

CHAPTER II

PRIMITIVE MYTHOLOGY

Chapter II

For, indeed. in the primitive world, where most of the clues to the origin of mythology must be sought, the gods and demons are not conceived in the way of hard and fast, positive realities. A god can be simultaneously in two or more places -- like a melody, or like the form of a traditional mask. And wherever he comes, the impact of his presence is the same: it is not reduced through multiplication. Moreover, the mask in a primitive festival is revered and experienced as a veritable apparition of the mythical being that it represents -- even though everyone knows that a man made the mask and that a man is wearing it. The one wearing it, furthermore, is identified with the god during the time of the ritual of which the mask is a part. He does not merely represent the god; he IS the god. (MPM, p. 21)

Our first tangible evidences of mythological thinking are from the period of Neanderthal Man, which endured from ca. 250,000 to ca. 50,000 B.C.; and these comprise, first, burials with food supplies, grave gear, tools sacrificed animals, and the like; and second, a number of chapels in high-mountain caves, where cavebear skull, ceremonially disposed in symbolic settings, have been preserved. The burials suggest the idea, if not exactly of immortality, then at least of some kind of life to come; and the almost inaccessible high-mountain bear-skull sanctuaries surely represent a cult in honor of that great, upright, manlike, hairy personage, the bear. The bear is still revered by the hunting and fishing peoples of the far North, both in Europe and Siberia and among our North American Indian tribes; and we have reports of a number among whom the heads and skulls of the honored beasts are preserved very much as in those early Neanderthal caves. (MLB, p. 31)

Among the earliest evidence we can cite today of emergent manlike creatures on this earth are the relics recently unearthed in the Olduvai Gorge of East Africa by Dr. L. S. B. Leakey: distinctly humanoid jaws and skulls discovered in earth strata of about 1,800,000 years ago. That is a long, long drop into the past. And from that period on, until the rise in the Near East of the arts of grain agriculture and domestication of cattle, man was dependent absolutely for his food supply on foraging for roots and fruit and on hunting and fishing. In those earliest millenniums, furthermore, men dwelt and moved about in little groups as a minority on this earth. (MLB, p. 30)

The rugged race and life style of Neanderthal Man passed away and even out of memory with the termination of the Ice Ages, some forty thousand years ago; and there appeared then, rather abruptly, a distinctly superior race of man, Homo sapiens proper, which is directly ancestral to ourselves. It is with these men -- significantly -- that the beautiful cave paintings are associated with the French Pyrenees, French Dordogne, and Spanish Cantabrian hills; also, those little female figurines of stone, or of mammoth bone or ivory, that have been dubbed -- amusingly -- paleolithic Venuses and are, apparently, the earliest works ever produced of human art. (MLB, pp. 35-36)

And it seems to me important to remark that, whereas when masculine figures appear in the wall paintings of the same period they are always clothed in some sort of costume, these female figurines are absolutely naked, simply standing, unadorned. This says something about the psychological and consequently mythical values of, respectively, the male and the female presences. The woman is immediately mythic in herself giver of life, but also in the magic of her touch and presence. The accord of her seasons with the cycles of the moon is a matter of mystery too. Whereas the male, costumed, is one who has gained his powers and represents some specific, limited, social role of function. In infancy--as both Freud and Jung have pointed out--the mother is experienced as a power of nature and the father is the authority of society. (MLB, p. 36)

The comparative study of the mythologies of the world compels us to view the cultural history of mankind as a unit; for we find that such themes as the fire-theft, deluge, land of the dead, virgin birth, and resurrected hero have a worldwide distribution--appearing everywhere in new combinations while remaining, like the elements of a kaleidoscope, only a few and always the same. Furthermore, whereas in tales told for entertainment such mythical themes are taken lightly--in a spirit, obviously, of play--they appear also in religious contexts, where they are accepted not only as factually true but even as revelations of the varieties to which the whole culture is a living witness and from which it derives both spiritual authority and its temporal power. No human society has yet been found in which such mythological motifs have not been rehearsed in liturgies; interpreted by seers, poets, theologians, or philosophers, presented in art; magnified in song; and ecstatically experienced in life-empowering visions. (MPM, p. 3)

Certain imprints impressed upon the nervous system in the plastic period between birth and maturity are the source of many of the most widely known images of myth. Necessarily the same for all mankind, they have been variously organized in the differing traditions, but everywhere function as potent energy releasers and directors. (MPM, p. 61)

It is already clear from the studies that have been made of children in the West--who are the only ones that have been systematically examined--that the rational logic and scientific views that ultimately replace in their thinking the spontaneous animistic and artificialist theories of infancy only gradually suppress or dissolve the earlier notions. Names are not correctly distinguished from their referents until somewhere about the tenth or eleventh year. Life becomes restricted to animals and plants, and consciousness to animals, hardly before the ages of eleven or twelve. And yet even after the basic laws of physics and chemistry have been learned, which have been so painfully drawn from nature by the long toil of science, when the adult is asked about the mysteries of creation it is seldom that he will answer in other terms than those of the infantile artificialist or animist: the world has been made by some omniscient god for some purpose, and we for some end, which we must learn to know and to serve, or else--in replies somewhat more sophisticated--there is within things themselves some force that makes them, and immanent power out of which they arise and back into which they go. (MPM, p. 87)

The transformation of the child into the adult, which is achieved in higher societies through years of education, is accomplished on the primitive level more briefly and abruptly by means of the puberty rites that for many tribes are the most important ceremonials of the religious calendar. (MPM, p. 88)

But there is another aspect to this great world of the men's rites, for which no merely psychological reading of their symbolism can adequately account; namely, the particular mythological field to which the boy's intellect is being introduced. His crude energies of love and aggression are being broken from their primary spheres of reference and reorganized for manhood; but the particular system of imagery through which this psychological transformation is being effected has been determined not exclusively by general psychological laws, but also, and perhaps equally, by the particular social concerns of the local group. (MPM, p. 100)

It may be said that in the education of the young it has been the general custom in traditionally based societies to reorganize the common human inheritance of infantile imprints in such a way as to conduct the energies of the psyche from the primary system of references of infantile dependency into the sphere of the chief concerns of the local groups, but that in this developed reorganization of the primary symbols certain motifs appear that cannot be convincingly described as infantile and yet are not exclusively local either.   Throughout the world the rituals of transformation from infancy to manhood are attended with, and effected by, excruciating ordeals. Scourgings, fastings, the knocking out of teeth, scarifications, finger sacrifices, the removal of a testicle, cicatrization, circumcision, subincision, bitings, and burnings are the general rule. These, indeed, make brutally actual a general infantile fantasy of Oedipal aggression; but there is an additional aspect of the situation to be considered, inasmuch as the natural body is transformed by the ordeals into an ever-present sign of a new spiritual state. (MPM, p. 117)

Pleasure, power, and duty; these are the systems of reference of all experience on the natural level of the primitive societies.   And when such societies are in form, the first two are subordinated to the last, which, in turn, is mythologically supported and ritually enforced. Ritual is mythology made alive, and its effect is to concert men into angels. For archaic man was not a man at all, in the modern, individualistic sense of the term, but the incarnation of a socially determined archetype. And it was precisely in the rites of initiation that his apotheosis was effected--with what cruel imprint of hermetic art we have now seen. (MPM, p. 118)

Death is foreshadowed by the first signals of old age, which appear even today too soon for pleasure. How much sooner in the primitive past! When the woman of forty-five was a hag and the warrior of fifty an arthritic cripple, when, moreover, disease and the accidents of the hunt and of battle were everyone's immediate experience, Death was a mighty presence who had to be faced boldly even within the safest sanctuary, and whose force had to be assimilated. (MPM, p. 118)

The interdependence of death and sex, their import as the complementary aspects of a single state of being, and the necessity of killing--killing and eating--for the continuance of this state of being, which is that of man on earth and of all things on earth, the animals, birds, and fish, as well as man-- this deeply moving, emotionally disturbing glimpse of death as the life of the living is the fundamental motivation supporting the rites around which the social structure of the early planting villages was composed. (MPM, p. 177)

The sanctification of the local landscape is a fundamental function of mythology. You can see this very clearly with the Navaho, who will identify a northern mountain, a southern mountain, an eastern mountain, a western mountain, and a central mountain. In a Navaho hogan, the door always faces east. The fireplace is in the center, which becomes a cosmic center, with the smoke coming up through the hole in the ceiling so that the scent of the incense goes to the nostrils of the gods. The landscape, the dwelling place, becomes an icon, a holy picture. Wherever you are, you are related to the cosmic order. (PM, p. 91)

Not all primitive peoples are fighters, and when we turn from the hunting and warring nomads of the ranging animal plains to the more substantially settled village peoples of the tropics--inhabiting a largely vegetable environment, where plant, not animal food has been forever the basic diet-- we might expect to find a relatively peaceable world, with little or no requirements for either a psychology or a mythology of warcraft. However, as already remarked in earlier chapters, there is a very strange prevailing belief throughout those tropical zones, based on the observation that in the vegetable world new life arises from decay, life springs from death, and that from the rotting of last year's growths new plants arise. Accordingly, the dominant mythological theme of many of the peoples of those regions supports the notion that through killing one increases life, and it is, in fact, exactly in those parts of the world that the most horrible and grotesque rituals of human sacrifice obtain even to this day, their inspiration being the notion that to activate life one kills. It is in those areas that the headhunt flourishes, the basic idea there being that before a young man who is to marry can beget a wife, he must take a life and bring back as trophy a head--which will be honored at the wedding, not regarded with disdain, but respectfully entertained, so to say, as the giver of the power of life to the children of this marriage, now to be conceived and born. (MLB, pp. 177-78)

I like to think of the year 1492 as marking the end--or at least the beginning of the end--of the authority of the old mythological systems by which the lives of men had been supported and inspired from time out of mind. Shortly after Columbus's epochal voyage, Magellan circumnavigated the globe. Shortly before, Vasco da Gamma had sailed around Africa to India. The earth was beginning to be systematically explored, and the old, symbolic, mythological geographies discredited. (MLB, p. 4)

CHAPTER III

RITUALS AND RELIGIONS

Chapter III

Society was there before you, it is there after you are gone, and you are a member of it. The myths that link you to your social group, tribal myths, affirm that you are an organ of the larger organism. Society itself is an organ of a larger organism, which is the landscape, the world in which the tribe moves. The main theme in ritual is the linking of the individual to a larger morphological structure than that of his own physical body. (PM, p. 72)

The function of ritual, as I understand it, is to give form to human life, not in the way of a mere surface arrangement, but in depth. In ancient times every social occasion was ritually structured and the sense of depth was rendered through the maintenance of a religious tone. Today, on the other hand, the religious tone is reserved for exceptional, very special, "sacred" occasions. And yet even in the patterns of our secular life, ritual survives. It can be recognized, for example, not only in the decorum of courts and regulations of military life, but also in the manners of people sitting down to table together. (MLB, p. 43)

The accent of the planting rites is on the group; that of the hunters, rather, on the individual--though even here, of course, the group does not disappear. Even among the hunters we have the people-- the dear people--who bow to one another politely, like brothers-in-law, but have comparatively little personal power. And these constitute, even on that level, a group from which the far more potent shamans stand apart. (MPM, p. 241)

On the primitive level there is no requirement, or even possibility, that a local tribal god should be required as lord of the entire world. Each group has simply its own lawgiver and patron; the rest of the world - if there is such a thing - can take care of itself under its own gods; for each people is supposed to have a divine lawgiver and patron of its own. (OCM, p. 431)

The rites of the primitive hunters are not supposed to have descended from an age of mythological ancestors. They are said to have come, for the most part, directly from the animals themselves - from just such Animal Masters, or Master Animals, as the buffalo bull of this legend. And they have been received by such people as dwell in the world today, possessed however of shaman power. The atmosphere of this mythology is not mystical, but magical and shamanistic. The girl, even without knowing it, had shaman power; the great bull, too, had shaman power: he jumped and was not killed like the rest; the magpie was a shaman. According to the view of these people such power exists among shamans and visionaries to this day and it is through them - not from the ancestors of mythological age - that the people have received their rites. (RMR, p. 15)

The hunt itself, therefore, is a rite of sacrifice, sacred, and not a rawly secular affair. And the dance and chant received from the buffalo themselves are no less a part of the technique of the hunt than the buffalo drive and acts of slaughter. Human sacrifice, such as we found in the plant-dominated, equatorial domain, where an identification of human destiny with the model of the vegetable world conduced to rites of death, decay, and fruitful metamorphosis, we do not find among hunters unless there has been some very strong influence from the other zone (as, for example, in certain rituals of the Pawnee). The proper sacrifice for the hunter is the animal itself, which through its death and return represents the play of the permanent substance or essence in the shadow-world of accident and chance. (MPM, p. 293)

The rituals of primitive initiation ceremonies are all mythologically grounded and have to do with killing the infantile ego and bringing forth an adult, whether it's the girl or the boy. It's harder for the boy than for the girl, because life overtakes the girl. She becomes a woman whether she intends it or not, but the little boy has to intend to be a man. At the first menstruation, the girl is a woman. The next thing she knows, she's pregnant, she's a mother. The boy first has to disengage himself from his mother, get his energy into himself, and then start forth. That's what the myth of "Young man, go find your father" is all about. In the ODYSSEY, Telemachus lives with his mother. When he's twenty years old, Athena comes and says, "Go find your father." That is the theme all through the stories. Sometimes it's a mystical father, but sometimes, as here in the ODYSSEY, it's the physical father. (PM, p. 138)

There's a major difference, as I see it, between a shaman and a priest. A priest is a functionary of a social sort. The society worships certain deities in a certain way, and the priest becomes ordained as a functionary to carry out that ritual. The deity to whom he is devoted is a deity that was there before he came along. But the shaman's powers are symbolized in his own familiars, deities of his own personal experience. His authority comes out of a psychological experience, not a social organization. (PM, pp. 99-100)

The priest is the socially initiated, ceremonially inducted member of a recognized religious organization, where he holds a certain rank and functions as the tenant of an office that was held by others before him, while the shaman is one who, as a consequence of a personal psychological crisis, has gained a certain power of his own. The spiritual visitants who came to him in vision had never been seen before by any other; they were his particular familiars and protectors. The masked gods of the Pueblos, on the other hand, the corn-gods and the cloud-gods, served by societies of strictly organized and very orderly priests, are the well-known patrons of the entire village and have been prayed to and represented in the ceremonial dances since time out of mind. (MPM, p. 231)

There have been systems of religion where the mother is the prime parent, the source. The mother is really a more immediate parent than the father because one is born from the mother, and the first experiences of any infant is the mother. I have frequently thought that mythology is a sublimation of the mother image. We talk of Mother Earth. And in Egypt you have the Mother Heavens, the Goddess Nut, who is represented as the whole heavenly sphere. (PM, p. 165)

In primal societies, there are teeth knocked out, there are scarifications, there are circumcisions, there are all kinds of things done. So you don't have your little baby body anymore, you're somebody else entirely...

When I was a kid, we wore short trousers, you know, knee pants. And then there was a great moment when you put on long pants. Boys now don't get that. I see five-year-olds walking around with long trousers. When are they going to know that they're now men and must put aside childish things? (PM, p. 8)

The peculiar interests of adulthood differ radically form one society to another, and since it is a primary function of myth and ritual in traditional societies to shape youngsters into adults and them to hold the adults to their given roles, mythology and ritual, in as far as they serve this local, moral, ethical aim, cannot be called functions of any generally valid human psychology, but only of local history and sociology. (RMR, p. 47)

I was brought up as a Roman Catholic. Now, one of the great advantages of being brought up a Roman Catholic is that you're taught to take myth seriously and to let it operate on your life and to live in terms of these mythic motifs. I was brought up in terms of the seasonal relationships to the cycle of Christ's coming into the world, teaching in the world, dying, resurrecting, and returning to heaven. The ceremonies all through the year keep you in mind of the eternal core of all that changes in time. Sin is simply getting out of touch with that harmony...

And then I fell in love with the American Indians because Buffalo Bill used to come to Madison Square Garden every year with his marvelous Wild West Show. And I wanted to know more about Indians. My father and mother were very generous parents and found what books were being written for boys about Indians at that time. So I began to read American Indian myths, and it wasn't long before I found the same motifs in the American Indian stories that I was being taught by the nuns at school. (PM, p. 10)

"Transcendent" is a technical, philosophical term, translated in two different ways. In Christian theology, it refers to God as being beyond or outside the field of nature. That is a materialistic way of talking about the transcendent, because God is thought of as a kind of spiritual fact existing somewhere out there. It was Hegel who spoke of our anthropomorphic god as a gaseous vertebrate - such an idea of God as many Christians hold. Or he is thought of as a bearded old man with a not very pleasant temperament. But "transcendent" properly means that which is beyond all concepts. Kant tells us that all of our experiences are bounded by time and space. They take place within space, and they take place in the course of time...

Time and space form the sensibilities that bound our experiences. Our senses are enclosed in the field of time and space, and our minds are enclosed in a frame of the categories of thought. But the ultimate thing (which is no thing) that we are trying to get in touch with is not so enclosed. We enclose it as we try to think of it...

The transcendent transcends all of these categories of thinking. Being and nonbeing -- those are categories. The word "God" properly refers to what transcends all thinking, but the word "God " itself is something thought about...

Now you can personify God in many, many ways. Is there one god? Are there many gods? Those are merely categories of thought. What you are talking and trying to think about transcends all that...

One problem with Yahweh, as they used to say in the Old Christian Gnostic texts, is that he forgot he was a metaphor. He thought he was a fact. And when he said "I am God," a voice was heard to say, "You are mistaken, Samael." "Samael" means "blind god": blind to the infinite Light of which he is a local historical manifestation. This is known as the blasphemy of Jehova -- that he thought he was God. (PM, p. 62)

When a judge walks into the room, and everybody stands up, you're not standing up to that guy, you're standing up to the robe that he's wearing and the role that he's going to play. What makes him worthy of that role is his integrity, as a representative of the principles of that role, and not some group of prejudices of his own. So what you're standing up to is a mythological character. I imagine some kings and queens are the most stupid, absurd, banal people you could run into, probably interested only in horses and women, you know. But you're not responding to them as personalities, you're responding to them in their mythological roles. When someone becomes a judge, or President of the United States, the man is no longer that man, he's the representative of an eternal office: he has to sacrifice his personal desires and even life possibilities to the role he now signifies. (PM, p. 12)

There is no doubt that in the twelfth and thirteenth centuries a major threshold of cultural change had been attained. The aims of the Christian conquest of Europe had been accomplished -- largely by force; the power of the papacy was at its height; the crusades were in full career; and yet from every side sounds and alarms of heresy were beginning to arise and to spread. The whole structure was cracking. For the cathedral of God's love, the Church, and the chalice of his divine blood -- the VAS of his self-giving on its altar -- had been turned frankly and openly to sheer force: the Church was a power state, a super power-state, and its image of God -- was a Levantine King of Kings in the perfect style of an Achaemenian Darius. (CM, p. 390)

The wicked thing about both the little and the great "collective faiths," prehistoric and historic, is that they all, without exception, pretend to hold encompassed in their ritualized mythologies all of the truth ever to be known. They are therefore cursed, and they curse all who accept them, with what I shall call the "error of the found truth," or, in mythological language, the sin against the Holy Ghost. They set up against the revelations of the spirit the barriers of their own petrified belief, and therefore, within the ban of their control, mythology, as they shape it, serves the end only of binding potential individuals to whatever system of sentiments may have seemed to the shapers of the past (now sanctified as saints, sages, ancestors, or even gods) to be appropriate to their concept of a great society. Thus, even a period of civilization that from without, and in the historian's view, would appear to be a golden age, might be a waste when viewed from within. (CM, p. 389)

With our old mythologically founded taboos unsettled by our own modern sciences, there is everywhere in the uncivilized world a rapidly rising incidence of vice and crime, mental disorders, suicides and dope addictions, shattered homes, imprudent children, violence, murder, and despair. These are facts; I am not inventing them. They give point to the cries of the preachers for repentance, conversion, and return to the old religion. And they challenge, too, the modern educator with respect to his own faith and ultimate loyalty. (MLB, p. 9)

The Buddhist Nirvana is a center of peace of this kind. Buddhism is a psychological religion. It starts with the psychological problem of suffering: all life is sorrowful; there is, however, from sorrow; the escape is Nirvana - which is a state of mind or consciousness, not a place somewhere, like heaven. It is right here, in the midst of the turmoil of life. It is the state you find when you are no longer driven to live by compelling desires, fears, and social commitments, when you have found your center of freedom and can act by choice out of that. (PM, p. 162)

The laws of the universe were of no interest in

themselves to the Buddhist seeker of the way out. There was no moral law derived from God; for there was no God, and the gods or principles by which the world was held in form were themselves the nets, traps and obstacles that the yogi must elude. (OCM, p. 247)

I have attended a number of psychological conferences dealing with this whole problem of the difference between the mystical experience and the psychological crack-up. The difference is that the one who cracks up is drowning in the water in which the mystic swims. You have to be prepared for this experience. (PM, p. 13)

What we're learning in our schools is not the wisdom of life. We're learning technologies, we're getting information. There's a curious reluctance on the part of faculties to indicate the life values of their subjects. In our sciences today - and this includes anthropology, linguistics, the study of religions, and so forth - there is a tendency to specialization. And when you know how much a specialist scholar has to know in order to be a competent specialist, you can understand this tendency. To study Buddhism, for instance, you have to be able to handle not only all the European languages in which the discussions of the Oriental come, particularly French, German, English, and Italian, but also Sanskrit, Chinese, Japanese, Tibetan, and several other languages. (PM, p. 9)

But now, finally, what would the meaning be of the word "truth" to a modern scientist? Surely not the meaning it would have for a mystic! For the really great and essential fact about the scientific revelation -- the most wonderful and most challenging fact -- is that science does not and cannot pretend to be "true" in any absolute sense. It is a tentative organization of mere "working hypotheses" ("Oh, those scientists!" "Yes, I know, but they found the bones") that for the present appear to take into account all the relevant facts now known. (MLB, p. 16)

CHAPTER IV

TRADITIONAL MYTHOLOGY

Our way of thinking in the West sees God as the final source or cause of the energies and wonder of the universe. But in most Oriental thinking, and in primal thinking, also, the gods are rather manifestations and purveyors of an energy that is finally impersonal. They are not its source. The god is the vehicle of its energy. And the force or quality of the energy that is involved or represented determines the character and function of the god. There are gods of violence, there are gods of compassion, there are gods that unite the two worlds of the unseen and the seen. and there are the gods that are simply the protectors of kings or nations in their war campaigns. These are all the personifications of the energies in play. But the ultimate source of the energies remains a mystery. (PM, pp. 207-208)

But now -- and here, I believe, as a point of fundamental importance for our reading of the basic difference between the Oriental and Occidental approaches to the cultivation of the soul -- in the Indian myth the principle of ego, "I" (aham), is identified completely with the pleasure principle, whereas in the psychologies of both Freud and Jung its proper function is to know and relate to external reality

(Freud's "reality principle"): not the reality of the metaphysical but that of the physical, empirical sphere of time and space. In other words, spiritual maturity, as understood in the modern Occident, requires a differentiation of ego from id, whereas in the Orient, throughout the history at least of every teaching that has stemmed from India, ego, (aham-kara: "the making of the sound 'I' ") is impugned as the principle of libidinous delusion, to be dissolved. (ORM, p. 15)

In the European West, on the other hand, where the fundamental doctrine of the freedom of the will essentially dissociates each individual from every other, as well as from both the will in nature and the will of God, there is placed upon each the responsibility of coming intelligently, out of his own experience and volition, to some sort of relationship with -- not identify with or extinction -- the all, the void, the suchness, the absolute, or whatever the proper term may be for that which is beyond terms. And, in the secular sphere likewise, it is normally expected that an educated ego should have developed away from the simple infantile polarity of the pleasure and obedience principles toward a personal, uncompulsive, sensitive relationship to empirical reality, a certain adventurous attitude toward the unpredictable, and a sense of personal responsibility for decisions. Not life as a good soldier, but life as a developed, unique individual, is the ideal. And we shall search the Orient in vain for anything quite comparable. There the ideal, on the contrary, is the quenching, not development, of ego. That is the formula turned this way and that, up and down the line, throughout the literature: a systematic, steady, continually drumming devaluation of the "I" principle, the reality function -- which has remained, consequently, undeveloped, and so, wide open to the seizures of completely uncritical mythic identifications. (ORM, pp. 22-23)

It is not easy for Westerners to realize that the ideas recently developed in the West of the individual, his selfhood, his rights, and his freedom, have no meaning whatsoever in the Orient. They had no meaning for primitive man. They would have meant nothing to the peoples of the early Mesopotamian, Egyptian, pugnant to ideals, the aims and orders of life, of most of the peoples of this earth. And yet - here is my second point -- they are the truly great " new thing" that we do indeed represent to the world and that constitutes our Occidental revelation of a properly human spiritual ideal, true to the highest potentiality of our species. (MLB, p. 61)

The use of visions to lead the mind and sentiments beyond themselves, over the thresholds to new realms of realization, has been developed in the Orient during the centuries since the writing of the "Guide Book to Meditation on Amida" into an extremely versatile pedagogical technique; and in its service not only books of meditation, but also works of visual art are employed. We have not yet, in our present systematic survey, arrived at the period of the greatest unfoldment of this visionary methodology. However, the basic principles are already evident.   (ORM, p. 313)

A Shinto rite, then, can be defined as an occasion for the recognition and evocation of an awe that inspires gratitude to the source and nature of being. And as such, it is addressed as art (music, gardening, architecture, dance, etc.) to the sensibilities - not to the faculties of definition. So that living in gratitude and awe amid the mystery of things. And to retain this sense, the faculties remain open, clean, and pure. That is the meaning of ritual purity. (ORM, p. 477)

In Zen, on the other hand, which in the period of its introduction to Japan became the Buddhism of the samurai, and essentially non-theological view is taken of the problem of illuminated life. All things are Buddha things. Buddhahood is within. Look within, the Buddha will be found. Act in this orientation and Buddhahood will act.   Freedom ("self-motivation," "spontaneity") is itself the manifestation of the Solar Buddha, which egoity, anxiety, fear, forcing, reasoning, etc., only impede, distort, and block. (ORM, p. 494)

In any case, the final point that I would make in this brief survey of the functioning and transformations of mythology in Japan, is that in the course of four grim centuries of feudal disintegration, there was produced, as from a highly fired kiln, an extraordinary glass-hard yet intensely poignant civilization, wherein the qualities of the entire religious inheritance of the Far East have become transmuted to secular ends. The world feeling of Shinto, that the processes of nature cannot be evil, together with its zeal for purity, and the clean house as well as the heart, where the processes become manifest unencumbered: the recognition of ineffable wonder in little things, and then the Buddhist lesson of the Flower Wreath that all is one and one is all, mutually arising - which adds to the Shinto mystique a magnitude: the Taoist feeling for the order of nature and Confucian for the Tao in human relationships, along with the Buddhist of the One Way that all things are following to the Buddhahood that is already theirs. (ORM, p. 502)

Throughout the dark green jungles of the world there abound not only dreadful animal scenes of tooth and claw, but also terrible human rites of cannibal communion, dramatically representing -- with the force of an initiatory shock -- the murder scene, sexual act, and festival meal of the beginning, when life and death became two, which had been one, and the sexes became two, which had also been one. Creature come into being, live on the death of others, die, and become the food of others, continuing, thus into and through the transformations of time, the timeless arche-type of the mythological beginning; and the individual matters no more than a fallen leaf. Psychologically, the effect of the enactment of such a rite is to shift the focus of the mind from the individual (who perishes) to the everlasting group. Magically, it is to reinforce the ever-living life in all lives, which appears to be many but is really one; so that the growth is stimulated of the yams, coconuts, pigs, moon, and breadfruits, and of the human community as well. (ORM, p. 4)

Moving still farther eastward, to China and Japan, we come to another cluster of mythologies of peace, particularly of Lao-tzu and Confucius. Many would term the founding through of these mythologies romantic; for it is simply that there is through all of nature an all-suffusing spiritual harmony: an orderly interaction through all life and lives, through all history and historical institutions, of those two principles or powers, active and passive, light and dark, hot and cold, heavenly and earthly, known as YANG and YIN, later and increasingly in old age. YANG is dominant in summer, in the south, and at noon; YIN in winter, in the north, and at night. The way of their alternations through all things is the Way of all things, the TAO -- one's time, one's world, oneself -- one accomplishes the ends of life and is at peace in the sense of being in harmony with all things. (MLB, p. 197)

Whereas the typical Occidental hero is a personality, and therefore necessarily tragic, doomed to be implicated seriously in the agony and mystery of temporality, the Oriental hero is the monad: in essence without character but an image of eternity, untouched by, or else casting off successfully, the delusory involvements of the mortal sphere. And just as in the West the orientation to personality is reflected in the concept and experience even of God as a personality, so in the Orient, in perfect contrast, the overpowering sense of an absolutely impersonal law suffusing and harmonizing all things reduces to mere blot the accident of an individual life. (ORM, p. 243)

Buddhism cannot be taught. What are taught are simply the ways that lead from various points of the spiritual compass to the Bodhi-tree; and to know those ways is not enough. To see the tree is not enough. Even to go sit beneath the tree is not enough. Each has to find and sit beneath thetree himself and then, in solitary thought, begin the passage into and to himself, who is nowhere at all. (ORM, p. 274)

The myth of eternal return, which is still basic to Oriental life, displays an order of fixed forms that appear and reappear through all time. The daily round of the sun, the waning and waxing moon, the cycle of the year, and the rhythm or organic birth, death, and new birth, represent a miracle of continuous arising that is fundamental to the nature of the universe. (ORM, p. 3)

The world is full of origin myths, and all are factually false. The world is full, also, of great traditional books tracing the history of man (but focused narrowly on the local group) from the age of mythological beginnings, through periods of increasing plausibility, to a time almost within memory, when the chronicles begin to carry the record, with a show of rational factuality, to the present. Furthermore, just as all primitive mythologies serve to validate the customs, systems of sentiments, and political aims of their respective local groups, so do these great traditional books. On the surface they may appear to have been composed as conscientious history.   In depth they reveal themselves to have been conceived as myths: poetic readings of the mystery of life from a chronicle of fact is - to say the least - to miss the point. To say a little more, it is to prove oneself a dolt. And to add to this, the men who put these books together were not dolts but knew precisely what they were doing - as the evidence of their manner of work reveals at every turn. (OCM, p. 95)

The high function of Occidental myth and ritual, consequently, is to establish a means of relationship - of God to Man and Man to God.   Such means are furnished, furthermore, by institutions, the rules of which cannot be learned through any scrutiny of nature, whether inward or without. Supernaturally revealed, these have come from God himself, as the myth of each institution tells; and they are administered by his clergy, in the spirit of the myth. (OCM, p. 4)

The geographical divide between the Oriental and Occidental ranges of myth and ritual is the tableland of Iran. Eastward are the two spiritual provinces of India and the Far East; westward, Europe and the Levant. (OCM, p. 3)

The best part of the Western tradition has included a recognition of and respect for the individual as a living entity.   The function of the society is to cultivate the individual. It is not the function of the individual to support society. (PM, p. 192)

In the Oriental metaphor, if you die in that condition, you come back again to have more experiences that will clarify, clarify, clarify, until you are released from these fixations. The reincarnating monad is the principal hero of Oriental myth. The monad puts on various personalities, life after life. Now the reincarnation idea is not that you and I as the personalities that we will be reincarnated. The personality is what the monad throws off. Then the monad puts on another body, male or female, depending on what experiences are necessary for it to clear itself of this attachment to the field of time.   (PM, p. 58)

This, I believe, is the great Western truth: that each of us is a completely unique creature and that, if we are ever to give any gift to the world, it will have to come out of our own experiences and fulfillment of our own potentialities, not someone else's. In the traditional Orient, on the other hand, and generally in all traditionally grounded societies, the individual is cookie-molded. His duties are put upon him in exact and precise terms, and there's no way of breaking out of them.   (PM, p. 151)

Ours is one of the worst histories in relation to the native peoples of any civilized nation. They are nonpersons. They are not even reckoned in the statistics of the voting population of the United States. There was a moment shortly after the American Revolution when there were a number of distinguished Indians who actually participated in American government and life. George Washington said that Indians should be incorporated as members of our culture. But instead, they were turned into vestiges of the past. In the nineteenth century, all the Indians of the southeast were put into wagons and shipped under military guard out to what was then called Indian Territory, which was given to the Indians in perpetuity as their own world - then a couple of years later was taken away from them. (PM, p. 13)

What, then, is the Waste Land? It is the land where the myth is patterned by authority, not emergent from life; where there is no poet's eye to see, no adventure to be lived, where all is set for all and forever: Utopia! Again, it is the land where poets languish and priestly spirits thrive, whose task it is only to repeat, enforce, and elucidate cliches. And this blight of the soul extends today from the cathedral close to the university campus. (CM, p. 373)

CHAPTER V

CREATIVE MYTHOLOGY

Chapter V

In the context of a traditional mythology, the symbols are presented in socially maintained rites, through which the individual is required to experience, or will pretend to have experienced, certain insights, sentiments, and commitments. In what I am calling "creative" mythology, on the other hand , this order is reversed: the individual has had an experience of his own - of order, horror, beauty, or even mere exhilaration - which he seeks to communicate through signs; and if his realization has been of a certain depth and import, his communication will have the value and force of living myth - for those, that is to say, who receive and respond to it of themselves, with recognition, uncoerced. (CM, p. 4)

The altogether new thing in the world that was making all the trouble was the scientific method of research, which in that period of Galileo, Kepler, Descartes, Harvey, and Francis Bacon was advancing with enormous strides. All walls, all the limitations, all the certainties of the ages were in dissolution, tottering. There had never been anything like it. In fact this epoch, in which we are participating still, with continually opening vistas, can be compared in magnitude and promise only to that of the eighth to fourth millenniums B.C.: of the birth of civilization in the nuclear Near East, when the inventions of food production, grain agriculture and stockbreeding, released mankind from the primitive conditions of foraging and so made possible an establishment of soundly grounded communities: first villages, then towns, then cities, kingdoms, and empires. (CM, pp. 29-30)

Now it has been - as I have already said - chiefly to the scientific method of research that this release of mankind has been due, and along with mankind as a whole, every developed individual has been freed from the once protective but now dissolved horizons of the local land, local moral code, local modes of group thought and sentiment, local heritages of signs. But this scientific method was itself a product of the minds of already self-reliant individuals courageous enough to be free. Moreover, not only in the sciences but in every department of life the will and courage to credit one's own senses and to honor one's own decisions, to name one's own virtues and to claim one's own vision of truth, have been the generative forces of the new age, the enzymes of the fermentation of the wine of this great modern harvest - which is a wine, however, that can be safely drunk only by those with a courage of their own. (CM, p. 30)

And just as in the past each civilization was the vehicle of its own mythology, developing in character as its myth became progressively interpreted, analyzed, and elucidated by its leading minds, so in this modern world - where the application of science to the fields of practical life has now dissolved all cultural horizons, so that no separate civilization can ever develop again - each individual is the center of a mythology of his own, of which his own intelligible character is the Incarnate God, so to say, whom his empirically questing consciousness is to find. (CM, p. 37)

For those who can still contrive to live within the fold of a traditional mythology of some kind, protection is still afforded against the dangers of an individual life; and for many the possibility of adhering in this way to established formulas is a birthright they rightly cherish, since it will contribute meaning and nobility to their unadventured lives, from birth to marriage and its duties and, with the gradual failure of powers, a peaceful passage of the last gate. (CM, p. 37)

Traditional mythologies, that is to say, whether of the primitive or of the higher cultures, antecede and control experience; whereas what I am here calling Creative Mythology is an effect and expression of experience. Its producers do not claim divine authority for their human, all too human, works. They are not saints or priests but men and women of this world; and their first requirement is that both their works and their lives should unfold from convictions derived from their own experience. (CM, p. 65)

In the primitive and Oriental provinces of collective authority and faith, local customs were always mythologically overinterpreted as of superhuman origin. Among the primitives, generally, the mythological ancestors in the mythological age were believed to have founded, once and for all, the customs by which their descendants would have to abide if they and the world itself were to endure. (CM, p. 87)

Shakespeare said that art is a mirror held up to nature. And that's what it is. The nature is your mirror, and all of these wonderful poetic images of mythology are referring to something in you. When your mind is simply trapped by the image out there so that you never make the reference to yourself, you have misread the image...

The inner world is the world of your requirements and your energies and your structure and your possibilities that meets the outer world. And the outer world is the field of your incarnation. That's where you are. You've got to keep both going. As Novalias said, "The seat of the soul is there where the inner and outer worlds meet." (PM, p. 57)

Let's say you are going to become fully human. In the first few years you are a child, and that is only a fraction of the human being. In a few more years you are in adolescence, and that is certainly a fraction of the human being. In maturity you are still fractional - you are not a child, but you are not old yet. There is an image in the Upanishads of the original, concentrated energy which was the big bang of creation that set forth the world, consigning all things of time to the full power of original being - that is a function of art. (PM, p. 228)

This attitude toward art as an aspect of the game of life, and life itself as the art of a game, is a wonderfully joyous, invigorating approach to the mixed blessing of existence -- quite in contrast to this of our Christian West, based on a mythology of universal guilt. There was that Fall, back there, in the Garden, and we have all been congenital sinners ever since. Every act of nature is an act of sin, accompanied by knowledge of its guilt. Whereas in the Orient there is the ideas of the inherent innocence of nature, even in what might appear to our human eyes and sentiments to be its cruelties. (MLB, p. 126)

And so let me now cite, in illustration of the high service of ritual to a society, the very solemn state occasion that followed, in Washington, D.C., the assassination of President Kennedy. That was a ritualized occasion of the greatest social necessity. The nation as a unit had suffered a shocking loss, a loss that had been shocking in depth -- in a unanimous sense. No matter what one's opinions and feelings politically might have been, that magnificent young man representing our whole society, the living social organism of which ourselves were the members, taken away at the height of his career, at a moment of exuberant life -- suddenly death, and then the appalling disorder that followed: all this required a compensatory rite to reestablish the sense of solidarity of the nation, not only as an occasion for us, here, within the nation, but also as a statement for the world, of our majesty and dignity as a modern civilized state. I count the splendid performance of the radio and television companies at that critical time an integral part of the ritual of which I speak: it was one of the spontaneous, living aspects of the occasion. For here was an enormous national; yet during those four days it was made a unanimous community, all of us participating in the same way, simultaneously, in a single symbolic event. To my knowledge, this was the first and only thing of its kind in peacetime that has ever given me a sense of being a member of this whole national community, engaged as a unit in the observance of a deeply significant rite. (MLB, pp. 52-53)

The reader hardly need be reminded that the images not only of poetry and love but also of religion and patriotism, when effective, are apprehended with actual physical responses: tears, sighs, interior aches, spontaneous groans, cries, bursts of laughter, wrath, and impulsive deeds. Human experience and human art, that is to say, have succeeded in creating for the human species an environment of sign stimuli that release physical responses and direct them to ends no less effectively than do the signs of nature the instincts of the beasts. The biology, psychology, sociology, and history of these sign stimuli may be said to constitute the field of our subject, the science of Comparative Mythology. (MPM, p. 41)

The Oriental artist must not only address himself to standard themes, but also have not interest in any such thing as we understand by self expression. Accounts, such as abound in the biographies of Western masters, of an artist's solitary agony in long quest of his own special language to bring forward his personal message, we shall search for long and in vain in the annals of Oriental art. (MLB, p. 108)

The artist lives thus in two worlds - as do we all; but he, in so far as he knows what he is doing, in a special state of consciousness of this micromacrocosmic crucifixion that is life on earth and is perhaps, also, the fire of the sun, stars, and galaxies beyond. (CM, p. 333)

Freud's own thoughts about art and artists were already well known to Mann, no less than to anyone else in that room, and they were certainly not Mann's own. They had been stated on many occasions, and most sharply, sixteen years before, in a lecture on "The Paths of Symptom-Formation" that had been published as Lecture Twenty-three of Freud's General Introduction to Psychoanalysis. There we find the artist diagnosed (from the point of view of "useful cognition") as one who desires intensely "honor, power, riches, fame, and the love of women," but lacks the means to attain them. Frustrated, he becomes introverted and turns with unsatisfied longing from reality to fantasizing - which, in the Freudian view, is always unconsciously predetermined by represses infantile fears and desires. Since the artist, however, is gifted with what Freud in this passage terms the "mysterious ability" to reproduce his daydreams in such a way as to afford satisfaction to other frustrated souls, he earns their gratitude and admiration, and (to quote): "has won thus through fantasy what before he could win only in fantasy, namely, honor, power, and the love of women." (EI, p. 2)

Sit in a room and read and read -- and read and

read. And read the right books by the right people. Your mind is brought onto that level, and you have a nice, mild, slow-burning rapture all the time. This realization of life can be a constant realization in your living. When you find an author who really grabs you, read everything he has done. Don't say, "Oh, I want to know what So-and-so did" - and don't bother at all with the best seller list. Just read what this one author has to give you. And then you can go and read what he had read. And the world opens up in a way that is consistent with a certain point of view. But when you go from one author to another, you may be able to tell us the date when he wrote such and such a poem -- but he hasn't said anything to you. (PM, p. 99)

Anyone writing a creative work knows that you open, you yield yourself and the book talks to you and builds itself. To a certain extent, you become the carrier of something that is given to you from what have been called the Muses - or in biblical language, "God." This is no fancy, it is a fact. Since the inspiration comes from the unconscious, and since the unconscious minds of people of any single small society have much in common, what the shaman or seer brings forth is something that is waiting to be brought forth in everyone. So when one hears the seer's story, one responds, "Aha! This is my story. This is something that I had always wanted to say but wasn't able to say." There has to be a dialogue, an interaction between the seer and the community. The seer who sees things that people in the community don't want to hear is just ineffective. Sometimes they will wipe him out. (PM, pp. 58-59)

I don't know what's coming, any more than Yeats knew, but when you come to the end of one time and the beginning of a new one, it's a period of tremendous pain and turmoil. The threat we feel, and everybody feels - well, there is this notion of Armageddon coming. (PM, p. 17)

The big problem of any young person's life is to have models to suggest possibilities. Nietzsche says, "Man is the sick animal." Man is the animal that doesn't know what to do with itself. The mind has many possibilities, but we can live no more than one life. What are we going to do with ourselves? A living myth presents contemporary models. (PM, p. 150)

There is a magnificent essay by Schopenhauer in which he asks, how is it that a human being can so participate in the peril or pain of another that without thought, spontaneously, he sacrifices his own life to the other? How can it happen that what we normally think of as the first law of nature and self-preservation is suddenly dissolved?...

Schopenhauer's answer is that such a psychological crisis represents the breakthrough of a metaphysical realization, which is that you and that other are one, that you are two aspects of the one life, and that your apparent separateness is but an effect of the way we experience forms under the conditions of space and time. Our true reality is in our identity and unity with all life. This is a metaphysical truth which may become spontaneously realized under circumstances of crisis. For it is, according to Schopenhauer, the truth of your life. (PM, p. 110)

Schopenhauer, in his splendid essay called "On an Apparent Intention in the Fate of the Individual," points out that when you reach an advanced age and look back over your lifetime, it can seem to have had a consistent order and plan, as though composed by some novelist. Events that when they occurred had seemed accidental and of little moment turn out to have been indispensable factors in the composition of a consistent plot. So who composed that plot? Schopenhauer suggests that just as your dreams are composed by an aspect of yourself of which your consciousness is unaware, so, too, your whole life is composed by the will within you. And just as people whom you will have met apparently by mere chance became unknowingly as an agent, giving meaning to the lives of others.   The whole thing gears together like one big symphony, with everything unconsciously structuring everything else. And Schopenhauer concludes that it is as though our lives were the features of the one great dream of a single dreamer in which all the dream characters dream, too; so that everything links to everything else, moved by the one will to life which is the universal will in nature. (PM, p. 229)

For in Schopenhauer's view, the will, the will to life, which is the very Being of beings, is a blind, insatiable drive, motivating all and eventuating mainly in the sorrows and deaths of all - as anyone can see - yet willfully continued. The more strongly the will to life is affirmed, the more painful are its effects, not only in the willing subject, whose will for more is only enhanced by success, never quelled; but also, and even more hurtfully, in those round about him, whose equivalent wills he frustrates. For each of us in his own way, as Schopenhauer tells, is metaphysically and essentially the entire world as will, and consequently can be satisfied with nothing less than possession of the entire world as object, which, since everyone would have it so, is not possible to any. (CM, p. 357)

An altogether different approach is represented by Carl G. Jung, in whose view the imageries of mythology and religion serve positive, life-furthering ends. According to his way of thinking, all the organs of our bodies - not only those of sex and aggression - have their purposes and motives, some being subject to conscious control, others, however, not. Out outward-oriented consciousness, addressed to the demands of the day, may lose though with these inward forces; and the myths, states Jung, when correctly read, are the means to bring us back in touch. They are telling us in picture language of powers of the psyche to be recognized and integrated in our lives, powers that have been common to the human spirit forever, and which represent that wisdom of the species by which man has weathered the millenniums. Thus they have not been, and can never be, displaced by the findings of science, which relate rather to the outside world than to the depths that we enter in sleep. Through a dialogue conducted with these inward forces through our dreams and through a study of myths, we can learn to know and come to terms with the greater horizon of our own deeper and wiser, inward self. And analogously, the society that cherishes and keeps its myths alive will be nourished from the soundest, richest strata of the human spirit. (MLB, p. 13)

And so we may say in summary at this point that the first and absolutely essential characteristic of the new, secular mythology that was emerging in the literature of the twelfth and thirteenth centuries was that its structuring themes were not derived from dogma, learning, politics, or current concepts of the general social good, but were expressions of individual experience: what I have termed Libido as opposed to Credo. Undoubtedly the myths of all traditions, great and small, must have sprung in the first instance from individual experiences: indeed we possess, in fact, a world of legends telling of the prophets and visionaries through whose personal realizations the cults, sects, and even major religions of mankind were instituted. (CM, pp. 65-65)

James Joyce had been born a Catholic; Thomas Mann, a Protestant. Both had broken from their family spheres of belief in the ways fictionized in their first novels and short stories ("Stephen Hero," 1903, and A PORTRAIT OF THE ARTIST AS A YOUNG MAN, 1916; BUDDENBROOKS, 1902 and "Tonio Kroger," 1903); and each then cleared the way for himself - along parallel courses, at about the same pace, date for date - to an art of the most sophisticated psychologico-mythological ambiguities. Mann developed his position toward myth from Luther and Goethe, Schopenhauer, Wagner, and Nietzsche; Joyce, on the other hand, from the Middle Ages, Dante and Aquinas, Shakespeare, Blake, and then Ibsen. Consequently, although they were indeed on parallel courses, there were great differences between them in approach and aim as well as background, and with significant contrasts in result. (CM, p. 364)

Moreover, Joyce to the end retained an essentially priestly attitude toward the practice and function of his art; whereas Mann, the German Protestant, had the attitude, rather, of the preaching parson. The priest, saying Mass with his back to the congregation, is performing a miracle at his alter, much like that of the alchemist, bringing God himself into presence in the bread and wine, out of the nowhere into the here: and it matters not, to either God, the priest, the bread, or the wine, whether any congregation is present or not. The miracle takes place, and that is what the Mass, the opus, the act, is all about. Its effect is the salvation of the world. Whereas the preacher in his pulpit is addressing himself to people, to persuade them to some sort of life way, and if no one is present there is no event. Mann, accordingly, is writing to persuade. He explains, interprets, and evaluates discursively the symbols of his art, whereas Joyce simply presents, without author's comment. Furthermore, in his approach to symbols Mann comes to them from the secular world, through literature and art, not by way of the ingraining from childhood of the iconography of a seriously accepted, ritually ordered religion. (CM, p. 366)

And so now, in conclusion, let me return to that festival occasion of Thomas Mann's celebration of Freud. Exactly halfway through his Saturnalian talk he let fall the unutterable name; he named Jung. He protected himself by referring to the man as an "ungrateful scion of the Freudian school," which he must have known was untrue. Jung never studied under Freud, but was himself an authority on the psychology of schizophrenia when he met Freud in 1907, at the age of 32, and was immediately appointed Permanent President of the International Psychoanalytic Association. Moreover, it was not Jung who broke with Freud, but Freud who broke with Jung, when he realized that the younger man's psychology could never be identified with his own. Freud interpreted dreams as allegorical distortions of repressed infantile wishes, and when, in TOTEM AND TABU, he extended this view to the interpretation of myths and rites, he again looked back to infancy - now the infancy of the race - to explain the reference of their symbols. Jung, on the other hand, saw myth as symbolic, finally, not of occurrences in the past, but of the structures and powers of the psyche and consequently antecedent to history; and Mann saw them this way, too. Moreover, certain dreams (which Jung called "big dreams") might be interpreted, according to this view, as transcending personal experience and biography, pointing in the way of revelations to the great transpersonal mysteries of life and death, being, non-being, phenomenality and the like. (EI, p. 26)

Mann spoke of Jung as providing a bridge between occidental thought and oriental esoteric, and launched then into an open attack on Freud for his ignorance of philosophy and overestimation of his own science. All that science can do, Mann declared, is to write the Q.E.D. to some philosophical proposition; and those that Freud had demonstrated, whether knowingly or unknowingly, were of the great German Romantics: Novalis, Schopenhauer, Nietzsche, and so on; whereas Jung had enlarged on the insights of such thinkers through his understanding not only of oriental esoteric lore but also of the Greek and Egyptian hermetic mysteries. (EI, p. 27)

A dream is a personal experience of that deep, dark ground that is the support of our conscious lives, and a myth is the society's dream. The myth is the public dream and dream is the private myth. If your private myth, your dream, happens to coincide with that of the society, you are in good accord with your group. If it isn't, you've got an adventure in the dark forest ahead of you. (PM, p. 40)

On some levels a private dream runs into truly

mythic themes and can't be interpreted except by an analogy with a myth. Jung speaks of two orders of dream, the personal dream and the archetypal dream, or the dream of mythic dimension. You can interpret a personal dream by association, figuring out what it is talking about in your own life, or in relation to your own personal problem. But every now and then a dream comes up that is pure myth, that carries a mythic theme, or that is said, for example, to come from the Christ within. (PM, p. 42)

Archetype of the unconscious means it comes from below. The difference between the Jungian archetypes of the unconscious and Freud's complexes is that the archetypes of the unconscious are manifestations of the organs of the body and their powers. Archetypes are biologically grounded, whereas from the individual's lifetime. The Freudian unconscious is a personal unconscious, it is biographical. The Jungian archetypes of the unconscious are biological. The biographical is secondary to that. (PM, p. 51)

It is amazing, really, to think that in our present world with all its sciences and machines, megalopolitan populations, penetration of space and time, night life and revolutions, so different (it would seem) from the God-filled world of the Middle Ages, young people should still exist among us who are facing in there minds, seriously, the same adventure as thirteenth-century Gottfried: challenging hell. If one could think of the Western World for a moment in terms not of time but of space; not as changing in time, but as remaining in space, with the men of its various eras, each in his own environment, still there as contemporaries discoursing, one could perhaps pass from one to another in a trackless magical forest, or as in a garden of winding ways and little bridges. (CM, p. 38)

You must have a room, or a certain hour or so a day, where you don't know what was in the newspapers that morning, you don't know who your friends are, you don't know what you owe anybody, you don't know what anybody owes to you. This is a place where you can simply experience and bring forth what you are and what you might be. This is the place of creative incubation. At first you may find that nothing happens there. But if you have a sacred place and use it, something eventually will happen. (PM, p. 92)

The best things cannot be told, the second best are misunderstood. After that comes civilized conversation; after that, mass indoctrination; after that, intercultural exchange. And so, proceeding, we come to the problem of communication: the opening, that is to say, of one's own truth and depth to the depth and truth of another in such a way as to establish an authentic community of existence. (CM, p. 84)

CHAPTER VI

THE HERO'S JOURNEY AND BEYOND

Chapter VI

Each person can have his own depth, experience, and some conviction of being in touch with his own *sat-chit-ananda*, his own being through consciousness and bliss. The religious people tell us we really won't experience bliss until we die and go to heaven. But I believe in having as much as you can of this experience while you are still alive. (PM, p. 120)

Poets are simply those who have made a profession and a lifestyle of being in touch with their bliss. Most people are concerned with other things. They get themselves involved in economic and political activities, or get drafted into a war that isn't the one they're interested in, and it may be difficult to hold to this umbilical under those circumstances. That is a technique each one has to work out for himself somehow. (PM, pp. 118-119)

The quest to find the inward thing that you basically are is the story that I tried to render in that little book of mine written forty-odd years ago - THE HERO WITH A THOUSAND FACES. The relationship of myths to cosmology and sociology has got to wait for man to become used to the new world that he is in. The world is different today from what it was fifty years ago. But the inward life of man is exactly the same. So if you put aside for a while the myth of the origin of the world - scientists will tell you what that is, anyway - and go back to the myth of what is the human quest, what are its stages of realization, what are the trials of the transition from childhood to maturity and what does maturity mean, the story is there, as it is in all the religions. (PM, p. 139)

If the person insists on a certain program, and doesn't listen to the demands of his own heart, he's going to risk a schizophrenic crackup. Such a person has put himself off center. He has aligned himself with a program for life, and it's not the one the body's interested in at all. The world is full of people who have stopped listening to themselves or have listened only to their neighbors to learn what they ought to do, how they ought to behave, and what the values are that they should be living for. (PM, p. 147)

The moral objective is that of saving a people, or saving a person, or supporting an idea. The hero sacrifices himself for something - that's the morality of it. Now, from another position, of course, you might say that the idea for which he sacrificed himself was something that should not have been respected. That's a judgement from the other side, but it doesn't destroy the intrinsic heroism of the deed performed. (PM, p. 127)

Essentially, it might even be said there is but one archetypal mythic hero whose life has been replicated in many lands by many, many people. A legendary hero is usually the founder of something - the founder of a new age, the founder of a new religion, the founder of a new city, the founder of a new way of life. In order to found something new, one has to leave the old and go in quest of the seed idea, a germinal idea that will have the potentiality of bringing forth that new thing. (PM, p. 136)

The usual pattern is, first, of a break away or departure from the local social order and context; next, a long, deep retreat inward and backward, as it were, in time, and inward, deep into the psyche; a chaotic series of encounters there, darkly terrifying experiences, and presently (if the victim is fortunate) encounters of a certain kind, fulfilling, harmonizing, giving new courage; and then finally, in such fortunate cases, a return journey of rebirth to life. And that is the universal formula also of the mythological hero journey, which I, in my own published work, had described as: 1) separation, 2) initiation, and 3) return. (MLB, pp. 208-209)

In the mythological sense, he (John Lennon) was an innovator. The Beatles brought forth an art form for which there was a readiness. Somehow, they were in perfect tune with their time. Had they turned up thirty years before, their music would have fizzled out. The public hero is sensitive to the needs of his time. The Beatles brought a new spiritual depth into popular music which started the fad, let's call it, for meditation and Oriental music. Oriental music had been over here for years, as a curiosity, but now, after the Beatles, our young people seem to know what it's about. We are hearing more and more of it, and it's being used in terms of its original intention as a support for meditations. That's what the Beatles started. (PM, p. 134)

Just sheer life cannot be said to have a purpose, because look at all the different purposes it has all over the place. But each incarnation, you might say, has a potentiality, and the mission of life is to live that potentiality. How do you do it? My answer is, "Follow your bliss." There's something inside you that knows when you're in the center, that knows when you're on the beam or off the beam. And if you get off the beam to earn money, you've lost your life. And if you stay in the center and don't get any money, you still have your bliss. (PM, p. 229)

The state of the child in the womb is one of bliss, actionless bliss, and this state may be compared to the beatitude visualized for paradise. In the womb, the child is unaware of the alternation of night and day, or of any of the images of temporality. It should not be surprising, therefore, if the metaphors used to represent eternity suggest, to those trained in the symbolism of the infantile unconscious, retreat to the womb. (MPM, p. 65)

Otto Rank in his important little book THE MYTH OF THE BIRTH OF THE HERO declares that everyone is a hero in birth, where he undergoes a tremendous psychological as well as physical transformation, from the condition of a little water creature living in a realm of amniotic fluid into an air-breathing mammal which ultimately will be standing. That's an enormous transformation, and had it been consciously undertaken, it would have been, indeed, a heroic act. And there was a heroic act on the mother's part, as well, who had brought this all about. (PM, pp. 124-125)

You can't predict what a myth is going to be any more than you can predict what you're going to dream tonight. Myths and dreams come from the same place. They come from realizations of some kind that have then to find expression in symbolic form.. And the only myth that is going to be worth thinking about in the immediate future is one that is talking about the planet, and everybody on it. That's my main thought for what the future myth is going to be.

And what it will have to deal with will be exactly what all myths have dealt with - the maturation of the individual, from dependency through adulthood, through maturity, and then to the exit; and then how to relate to this society and how to relate this society to the world of nature and the cosmos. That's what the myths have all talked about, and what this one's got to talk about. But the society that it's got to talk about is the society of the planet. And until that gets going, you don't have anything. (PM, p. 32)

To predict what the imagery of the poetry of man's future is to be, is today, of course, impossible. However, those same three astronauts, when coming down, gave voice to a couple of suggestions. Having soared beyond thought into boundless space, circled many times the arid moon, and begun their long return: how welcome a sight, they said, was the beauty of their goal, this planet Earth, "like a oasis in the desert of infinite space!" Now there is a telling image: this earth, the one oasis in all space, an extraordinary kind of sacred grove, as it were, set apart for the rituals of life; and not simply one part or section of this earth, but the entire globe now a sanctuary, a set-apart Blessed Place. Moreover, we have all now seen for ourselves how very small is our heaven-born earth, and how perilous our position on the surface of its whirling, luminously beautiful orb. (MLB, pp. 244-245)

When you realize that if the temperature goes up fifty degrees and stays there, life will not exist on this earth, and that if it drops, let's say, another hundred degrees and stays there, life will not be on this earth; when you realize how very delicate this balance is, how the quantity of water is so important - well, when you think of all the accidents of the environment that have fostered life, how can you think that the life we know would exist on any other particle of the universe, no matter how many of these satellites around stars there may be? (PM, p. 17)

Automobiles have gotten into mythology. They have gotten into dreams. And airplanes are very much in the service of the imagination. The flight of the airplane, for example, is in the imagination as the release from earth. This is the same thing that birds symbolize, in a certain way. The bird is symbolic of the release of the spirit from bondage to the earth, just as the serpent is symbolic of the bondage to the earth. The airplane plays that role now. (PM, p. 18)

It is - and will forever be, as long as our human race exists - the old, everlasting, perennial mythology, in its "subjective sense," poetically renewed in terms neither of a remembered past nor of a projected future, but of now: addressed, that is to say, not to the flattery of "peoples," but to the waking of individuals in the knowledge of themselves, not simply as egos fighting for place on the surface of this beautiful planet, but equally as centers of Mind at Large - each in his own way at one with all, and with no horizons. (MLB, p. 275)

THE HERO'S JOURNEY TO BLISS

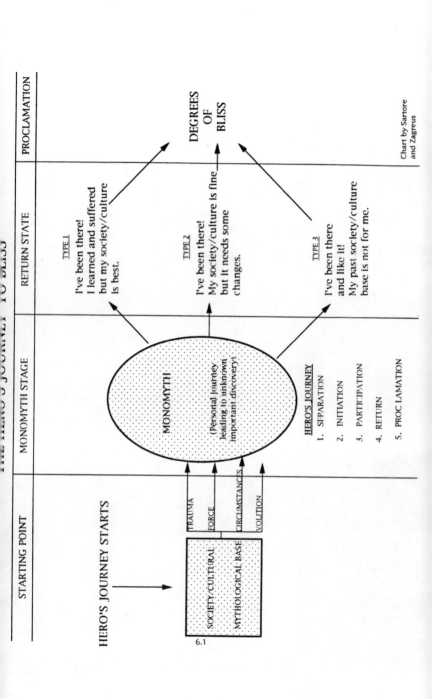

| STARTING POINT | MONOMYTH STAGE | RETURN STATE | PROCLAMATION |

HERO'S JOURNEY STARTS

SOCIETY/CULTURAL MYTHOLOGICAL BASE

6.1

TRAUMA
FORCE
CIRCUMSTANCES
VOLITION

MONOMYTH

(Personal journey leading to unknown important discovery)

HERO'S JOURNEY
1. SEPARATION
2. INITIATION
3. PARTICIPATION
4. RETURN
5. PROCLAMATION

TYPE 1

I've been there! I learned and suffered but my society/culture is best.

TYPE 2

I've been there! My society/culture is fine but it needs some changes.

TYPE 3

I've been there and like it! My past society/culture base is not for me.

DEGREES
OF
BLISS

Chart by Sartore and Zagreus

SYMBOLS FOR SOURCES

CM.................................. THE MASKS OF GOD: CREATIVE
                          MYTHOLOGY

EI .... EROTIC IRONY AND MYTHIC FORMS
                          IN THE ART OF THOMAS MANN

MPM............................. THE MASKS OF GOD: PRIMITIVE
                          MYTHOLOGY

MLB.............................. MYTHS TO LIVE BY

OCM.............................. THE MASKS OF GOD: OCCIDENTAL
                          MYTHOLOGY

ORM.............................. THE MASKS OF GOD: ORIENTAL
                          MYTHOLOGY

PM................................. THE POWER OF MYTH

RMR............................. RENEWAL MYTHS AND RITES OF THE
                          PRIMITIVE HUNTERS AND PLANTERS

* PAGE NUMBERS IN TEXT ARE DERIVED FROM REFERENCES
PROVIDED AT THE END OF THE BOOK.

CORRELATION OF MYTHIC THEMES WITH ERA

MYTHIC THEMES →

ERA OF MYTHOLOGY ↓	LIFE + DEATH		LOVE	RELIGION	SCIENCE	RITUAL	ART	LITERATURE	DREAMS	REINCARNATION / BLISS
PRIMITIVE MYTHOLOGY	p. 76	p. 71	p. 15	p. 33	p. 42	p. 30	p. 30	pp. 86-87	p. 62	p. 27
TRADITIONAL MYTHOLOGY	p. 17	pp. 32-33	pp. 49-50	p. 69	p. 39	p. 76	pp. 82-83	p. 86	p. 64	pp. 64-65
CREATIVE MYTHOLOGY	p. 17	p. 70	p. 47	p. 52	pp. 47-48	p. 73	p. 78	p. 86	p. 61	p. 95

* BY PAGE NUMBER IN TEXT

SELECT BIBLIOGRAPHY

Campbell, Joseph. AN OPEN LIFE. Larson Publications, New York: 1988.

Campbell, Joseph. EROTIC IRONY AND MYTHIC FORMS IN THE ART OF   THOMAS MANN.   Robert Briggs Associates, California: 1973.

Campbell, Joseph. THE FLIGHT OF THE WILD GANDER. Regnery Gateway,   Inc, Washington, D.C.: 1958.

Campbell, Joseph.   THE HERO WITH A THOUSAND FACES. Princeton   University Press, New Jersey: 1973.

Campbell, Joseph. HISTORICAL ATLAS OF WORLD MYTHOLOGY: VOLUME I -   THE WAY OF THE ANIMAL POWERS, PART 1 - MYTHOLOGIES OF THE PRIMITIVE HUNTERS AND GATHERERS. Harper & Row, Publishers,   New York: 1988.

Campbell, Joseph. HISTORICAL ATLAS OF WORLD MYTHOLOGY: VOLUME I -   THE WAY OF THE ANIMAL POWERS, PART 2 - MYTHOLOGIES OF THE GREAT   HUNT.   Harper & Row, Publishers, New York: 1988.

Campbell, Joseph. HISTORICAL ATLAS OF WORLD MYHTOLOGY: VOLUME II -   THE WAY OF THE SEEDED EARTH, PART 1 - THE SACRIFICE. Harper &   Row, Publishers, New York: 1988.

Campbell, Joseph. HISTORICAL ATLAS OF WORLD MYTHOLOGY: VOLUME II -   THE WAY OF THE SEEDED EARTH, PART 2 - MYTHOLOGIES OF THE PRIMITIVE PLANTERS: THE NORTHERN AMERICAS. Harper & Row,   Publishers, New York: 1989.

Campbell, Joseph. THE INNER REACHES OF OUTER SPACE. Harper & Row, Publishers, New York: 1986.

Campbell, Joseph. THE MASKS OF GOD: CREATIVE MYTHOLOGY. Penguin Books, New York: 1976.

Campbell, Joseph. THE MASKS OF GOD: ORIENTAL MYTHOLOGY. Penguin Books, New York: 1986.

Campbell, Joseph. THE MASKS OF GOD: PRIMITIVE MYTHOLOGY. Penguin Books, New York: 1986.

Campbell, Joseph. THE MYTHIC IMAGE. Princeton University Press, New Jersey: 1981.

Campbell, Joseph. MYTHS TO LIVE BY. Bantam Books, New York: 1984.

Campbell, Joseph (Conversation with Bill Moyers). THE POWER OF MYTH. Doubleday Publishing, New York: 1988.

Campbell, Joseph. RENEWAL MYTHS AND RITES OF THE PRIMITIVE HUNTERS AND PLANTERS. Spring Publication, Inc., Texas: 1989.

Campbell, Joseph (Edited with H.M. Robinson). A SKELETON KEY TO FINNEGANS WAKE. Viking Press, New York: 1977.

Campbell, Joseph. TRANSFORMATIONS OF MYTH THROUGH TIME. Harper & Row, Publishers, New York: 1989.

ABOUT THE AUTHOR

Richard L. Sartore holds a Bachelor and three Master degrees, one advanced degree from State University College at New Paltz and the remainder from State University of New York at Albany. Additional graduate work in education was completed at Albany. He has over fifteen years experience as a teacher, counselor and administrator on the elementary, secondary and university level. More than a hundred of his articles and poems, including the topic of mythology, appear in scholarly journals and magazines. Three years were spent as a Consulting Editor for the CLEARING HOUSE JOURNAL. Numerous writing awards include The Authors League Fund, Llewellyn Miller Fund and PEN American Center. He is currently a full time writer and Educational Consultant.